The Children's Book of
DOMESDAY ENGLAND

PETER B. BOYDEN

ILLUSTRATED BY

DAVID SALARIYA AND SHIRLEY WILLIS

Kingfisher Books

IN CONJUNCTION WITH THE
ENGLISH TOURIST BOARD

Contents

For Edmund and Elizabeth

The publishers wish to thank the following for supplying photographs for this book: 1 Collection Archives Nationales; 2 Colchester & Essex Museum; 3 Public Record Office (right); Ronald Sheridan (left); 6 Ronald Sheridan; 7 Michael Holford; 13 Public Record Office; 16 & 17 Royal Commission on Historical Monuments (England); 18 Public Record Office; 20 Michael Holford; 24 England Scene (top), Aerofilms (below); 26 Michael Holford; 32 J Allan Cash; 36 The Corporation of London Records Office (top); Ronald Sheridan (below); 39 Ronald Sheridan.

First published in 1985 by Kingfisher Books Limited
Elsley Court, 20–22 Great Titchfield Street, London W1P 7AD
A Grisewood & Dempsey Company

BRITISH LIBRARY CATALOGUING IN PUBLICATION DATA
Boyden, Peter B.
    The children's book of Domesday England.
    1. England – Social life and customs – Medieval period,
    1066–1485 – Juvenile literature
    I. Title
    942.02   DA185

ISBN 0-86272-154-7

Edited by Adrian Sington
Printed in Italy by Vallardi Industrie Grafiche, Milan

Above: A model of a Norman knight. He wears a coat of mail, called a *hauberk*, made of interlinked flat iron rings. The wooden shield covered with leather protects him from head to toe; and his heavy cutting sword has a long broad blade.

Right: The crypt of Winchester Cathedral. Wessex, the south western Anglo-Saxon kingdom, controlled most of England. Winchester was its capital and the centre of government.

Far right: The two volumes of Domesday Book open on the Domesday chest. Traditionally, Domesday Book was locked in this large chest which was kept in the Palace of Westminster, and afterwards in the Chapter House (see page 17). Made of wood, covered with iron, it was closed with three locks, the keys to which were held, for security reasons, by different officials.

Previous page: William I's seal

ntroduction

Open the pages of any modern atlas of England and many of the towns, villages, and manor houses marked on them are also mentioned in William the Conqueror's Domesday Book.

What is Domesday Book?

During the first seven months of 1086 a painstaking survey of England was carried out on William's orders. It was written in abbreviated Latin and Roman numerals. Although the ordinary people spoke the language we call Old English, and the King and his barons spoke Norman French, government records were written in Latin – the language of the church – because the men who wrote them were monks and priests. In any case, since most people, including the King, could not read at all it did not matter to them what language Domesday Book was written in.

The task of the Domesday commissioners, who collected the information, was to describe every manor in the country – what its tax assessment was, how many plough teams there were, and so on. In short, information which would give the best indication of the size, use and quality of the land holdings. The entries are arranged county by county, and within a county all the estates of each baron are listed together.

Although we speak about Domesday Book it is important to remember that Domesday 'Book' is two volumes. The larger one, Volume I, which describes most of the country, contains 382 pages of parchment, 43 cm by 28 cm in size. The other volume, describing only Essex, Norfolk and Suffolk, has 451 pages, but they are small, measuring 25.5 cm by 19 cm.

When it was compiled Domesday Book did not have a name, referring to itself as a *descriptio*, meaning a 'writing down'. The first proper name it had was the Book of Winchester, because it was kept in the Royal Treasury there. By 1170 it was popularly being called Domesday Book, because like the Day of Judgement – Doomsday – there could be no appeal against what it contained. Such was its importance that until the beginning of this century Domesday Book was being used in legal cases as the ultimate authority to settle disputes over the title to land.

Chapter

William's Reign

Duke William of Normandy became King of England by defeating the existing ruler, Harold II, at the Battle of Hastings in 1066. Although William claimed that he was the legitimate successor to Edward the Confessor, he had taken the throne by force, and frequently had to resort to the use of arms to keep it.

Opposition to William came from various sources. The sons of Harold, anxious to avenge their father's death, raided south west England from Ireland, gathering local support on the way. In 1067 William suppressed this rebellion at Exeter and built a castle there in an attempt to overawe the local population.

The most serious and longest threat to the Norman regime came from the Anglo-Saxon nobility. After Hastings many of them had sided with William and for this support had been allowed to keep their lands and positions. But they soon became dissatisfied with the loss of influence that they suffered through the appointment of foreigners to senior positions in church and state, and began to look for ways of overthrowing William.

In 1068 the northern earls rebelled. After brief skirmishes, the army restored control and William built castles at York, Lincoln, Warwick and other northern towns. But manned castles were not enough, and in the following year a general insurrection broke out in the north, supported by the Scots and the Danes. Danish ships in their hundreds (240, in fact) came to help the rebels. But William was more than a match for this force and by September 1069 he had sent them packing. In the winter of 1069, he decided to put paid to this unrest once and for all. In an operation that has come to be known as the 'Harrying of the North', he burnt and destroyed huge tracts of northern England. The savagery of this wholesale destruction was to trouble William's conscience later in his life, but it fulfilled its political purpose.

Further revolts came in 1071 at the hands of Hereward, who raised his standard in the Fens. Four years later another northern rebellion was suppressed by William's regents while he was in Normandy. For his part in it Earl Waltheof was executed in May 1076, the only English nobleman to suffer that fate.

Although the English opposition was now at an end, William also had to face trouble from within his own family. His eldest son Robert rebelled against his father in 1078 and 1083. He even had trouble from his half-brother Odo, Bishop of Bayeux, who was an important member of William's government. Yet the government continued to function efficiently despite all these problems; and it was this administrative backing that enabled William to embark on the completion of England's most famous public record – Domesday Book.

Plea of Penenden Heath near Maidstone, in 1072: this famous three-day sitting of the Kent shire court is being held a mile north of Maidstone to settle the case that Odo, Bishop of Bayeux (and also William's half-brother) held lands that were the rightful property of Canterbury Cathedral. The court found against Odo and the judgement marked the start of the church's recovery of lost land. The elderly man addressing the court is Aethelric, the former Bishop of Selsey. He had been a monk at

Canterbury in his youth, and has
been brought to the trial by
William's command to explain
points of the English law. He is so
weak he has to travel in a cart,
which is seen under the tree.
Behind Aethelric sit Odo (left) and
Lanfranc, the Archbishop of
Canterbury (right), with their
supporters. Facing them are the
jurors, and to their left the panel of
important men who conducted the
case, headed by Geoffrey, Bishop
of Coutances (standing). The rest
are English and French barons.

The Land – Who Owned What?

Domesday Book was an attempt to bring all the information on land tenure together and in so doing to sort out the outstanding disagreements over what land belonged to whom.

After the Battle of Hastings, William shared the lands of the Englishmen killed in the fighting among his supporters. As other Saxons died, or fled the country after the various rebellions, their estates were given away as well. So each Norman baron had one or more Saxon 'predecessors', whose estates and rights he took over. This system should have given rise to very few disputes over ownership, but the comings and goings of landowners to and from various rebellions in the first ten years of William's reign gave plenty of scope for the greedy to 'invade' and steal the land of their neighbours.

Theft was not the only problem. Before the Norman Conquest, the Abbey of Ely had leased land to people outside the church. When this land was given to William's supporters it deprived the monks of their land and, therefore, their rent. Enquiries were held to try and sort out whether Ely rightfully owned the land. It was finally resolved in 1080. But even after this, the abbey was still claiming estates held by others when the Domesday commissioners were collecting their information in 1086.

Above: The birthplace of William I. The small town of Falaise is dominated by its castle, perched dramatically on the cliff (*falaise* in French) above the river Ante. In the town below the castle William the Conqueror was born in the autumn of 1028, the bastard son of Duke Robert I of Normandy and Herlève, the seventeen-year-old daughter of Fulbert, a local tanner. The square keep of the castle dates from the 12th century, and to it the 35-metre tall Talbot Tower was added in the 15th century.

The situation at Ely was an extreme one, but similar enquiries were repeated all over the country. One of the most famous of these cases was the trial between Odo, Bishop of Bayeux, and Lanfranc, Archbishop of Canterbury, at Penenden Heath in 1072, which Odo lost (see previous page). After this case Odo is to be found all over the place presiding at various pleas. One in particular ended rather gruesomely. The case was a dispute between the Bishop of Rochester and the Sheriff of Cambridge over who owned Islesham manor. The jury of twelve found for the Bishop of Rochester, but Odo refused to accept this and appointed a second jury who gave a different verdict. Unfortunately, a Rochester monk gave information which proved that two members of the second jury had lied. The thoroughness and fairness of the courts in William's reign is shown by the fact that the original jury were sent to London to give evidence while the second had to plunge their right hands into boiling water *and* were heavily fined.

William's reign also saw the introduction of one of the most important aspects of the feudal system: the practice of knight service. Each knight in the kingdom was duty bound to follow his lord to war for 40 days of every year, armed and on horseback, and bringing with him some soldiers. In 1085, with a real threat

Below: Ely Cathedral seen from the south east. The abbey was the headquarters of one of the teams of commissioners collecting data for Domesday Book in 1086. After a troubled time during the first decades after the Norman Conquest, peace and prosperity returned to the Fenland monks. The rebuilding of the monastic church began in 1083, and the nave and western towers were completed during the 12th century, by which time Ely had been made the seat of a bishopric.

Above: Inhabitants of a village near the Essex coast leave their houses and move inland to escape from the threatened Danish invasion of 1085. On William's orders the villages and farms of the coastal districts are being laid waste so that if his enemies land they will find nothing to eat, or steal. The people are taking with them their livestock and some food, and of course their farm implements so that when they arrive at their new homes they can work and cultivate their own land. Because of the destruction and the upheaval that accompanied it, many people suffered a great deal of hardship during 1085. It is also an explanation for the decline in the population, livestock and value of some manors of north east Essex.

of a Danish invasion, there was every likelihood that the knights would very soon be heavily employed.

The Threat of Danish Invasion

In 1066 William became King of England by right of conquest. But there had been others with good claims to the throne. As a nephew of Cnut, who ruled England from 1016 to 1035, Sweyn Estrithson, King of Denmark (1047–1075) felt he had a strong claim, but he was much too busy trying to conquer Norway.

Sweyn's son Cnut succeeded his father as King of Denmark, and in 1085, after several unsuccessful attempts to take the

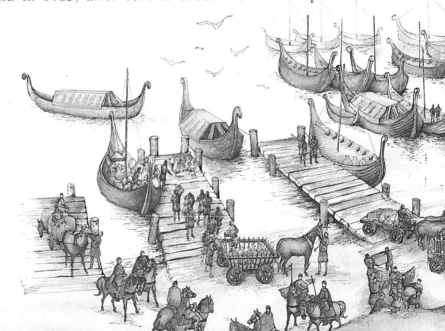

English throne, he finally decided to invade England with the help of his father-in-law, Count Robert of Flanders. When he first heard of the Danish preparations, William was in France. He returned to England with a huge army. Contemporary accounts talk of the Channel filled with ships stretching from coast to coast – it was quite simply the largest force ever to sail for England. But this time it was to protect her. The soldiers were billeted on William's barons all through the winter – the number of soldiers each had to billet being in proportion to the produce of his estate.

William took other measures to deal with the threatened Danish invasion. The *Anglo-Saxon Chronicle*, a history of England written up year by year, tells us that during 1085 people suffered terribly because the King ruined the land and had the crops in the coastal areas of the country destroyed to prevent the invaders from being able to live off the land. People had to leave their houses and move away from the coast for their own safety.

For whatever reason, having gone to these drastic lengths, the promised Danish invasion never happened and the huge army returned to France.

Below: The landing of Norman knights on the south coast in preparation for the Danish invasion. Stores, weapons, and armour are being unloaded from the flotilla of ships after the bulk of the fighting men and their horses have moved inland to their billets. On the clifftop the local sheriff and the leader of the troops supervise the work, while one of the sheriff's reeves (far right) leaves to take orders to the men on the jetty. Approaching them on foot are men carrying spears and a coat of chain mail. The long Norman boats have a mast to carry the square sail in use at the time, and oars which can be used when necessary. There are no cabins but tents are stretched across at night or during bad weather.

Chapter 2

The Council at Gloucester

In the wake of the upheavals caused by the threatened Danish invasion William spent Christmas 1085 at Gloucester. With the bishops and other senior churchmen, and the chief lay landholders of the country he held court, and 'much routine business affecting the nation's administration was transacted'. Then the clergy held a three-day synod, and, early in January 1086, the King had long and wide-ranging discussions with his councillors about the country that he had ruled for nearly twenty years. These talks showed that the King (and his government) had only a hazy idea of the social structure and distribution of wealth, so William decided to rectify this state of affairs. The first step was to send out teams of men (whom we call the Domesday commissioners) to collect details about his kingdom.

How Domesday was compiled

Two lists survive of the data that they were to find out. The *Anglo-Saxon Chronicle* recorded that the commissioners were to discover how many hides (taxable units) each shire contained, how much land and livestock the King himself held, and what revenue he received from it each year. They were also to record how much land each of his tenants-in-chief held, with details of their livestock and the values of their estates. The other list is to be found in a 12th-century account of the lands of the Abbey of Ely. This gives the items on the commissioners' questionnaire as the name of the estate, who held it in King Edward's time, who held it in 1086, how many hides it was assessed at, how many plough teams belonged to the lord, and how many to the tenants; how many villeins, cottars, slaves, freemen, and sokemen; how much wood, meadow, and pasture; how many mills, how many fisheries; how much had been added or taken away since 1066; how much each freeman or sokeman had there; and what the estate was worth. All of this information was to be given for three dates: in the time of King Edward, when the King gave it to the tenant-in-chief, and in 1086.

Left: The Royal Council meets in the Chapter House of Gloucester Abbey, early in January 1086 to hear William announcing his plans for the Domesday survey. While the King, on the throne in the apse, is in deep discussion with one of his advisers, groups of councillors, bishops and monks in the body of the room are holding their own conversations. Note the simplicity and beauty of the Norman arcade and stonework. The meeting takes place in mid-winter. Braziers and torches provide heat (and light) but because of the wooden roof none of the fires can be too fierce, so it is still very cold. To combat this the Norman barons wear a wool under-tunic, and sleeveless over-tunic open at the sides and belted. A cloak is secured at the shoulder with a brooch.

Preparing the information

The barons and churchmen who had been at the Gloucester council meeting returned home with the knowledge that a busy time lay ahead for the reeves and bailiffs who administered their estates. Soon after the meeting the King's chancery sent out instructions to the sheriff of each county, informing them of the information that was to be collected, and ordering them to have it available by a certain date. The sheriffs had lists of the manors in their shires, details of their current assessments, and the name of the person or institution responsible for paying the *geld* due.

Getting hold of this information was another matter. The ease with which the managers of the estates could supply the data depended on how well-organized the accounts were. In the case of monasteries and cathedrals, which had proper archives and well-run auditing and accounts sections, the details of all their estates were easily accessible. The larger barons had similar systems for administering their estates, although the extent of their records was limited by the fact that they had held their land for less than 20 years. At the end of the scale, a sokeman with a few acres of land could only describe his current circumstances, and perhaps recall those of his youth.

Above: Monks searching their monastery's archives for information on its estates to present to the Domesday commissioners. Royal diplomas giving the church land were often copied into Gospel Books, and one of these is to be seen on the table. It has a richer binding than the other volumes which contain surveys of estates and other records. The rolls are accounts prepared by bailiffs of the monks' manors, which contain details of changes in livestock, and money received from the sale of produce and from rents. In addition to checking facts on land that they actually possess, the monks also prepare claims to estates which they used to hold, but which were taken from them at the time of the Norman Conquest.

The Commissioners set out

Once the bulk of this statistical data had been prepared, the Domesday commissioners, accompanied by teams of clerks, set out to collect it. William's original plan was probably to send the county sheriffs out to collect the information; but as news of title disputes and other problems reached him, he decided to send out leading barons and churchmen as commissioners who could hear evidence and make a judgement on the spot.

There were seven groups of commissioners and the country was divided into seven circuits. They were: 1. Kent, Surrey, Sussex, Hampshire, and Berkshire. 2. Wiltshire, Dorset, Somerset, Devon, and Cornwall. 3. Gloucestershire, Herefordshire, Worcestershire, Shropshire, and Cheshire. 4. Oxfordshire, Warwickshire, Staffordshire, Leicestershire, and Northamptonshire. 5. Cambridgeshire, Bedfordshire, Hertfordshire, Middlesex, and Buckinghamshire. 6. Huntingdonshire, Derbyshire, Nottinghamshire, Yorkshire, and Lincolnshire. 7. Essex, Suffolk, and Norfolk.

As a matter of interest, we only know the names of one set of commissioners: those that visited Worcestershire and presumably the rest of the counties on that circuit. They were Remigius, Bishop of Lincoln, Walter Giffard, Henry de Ferrers, and Adam brother of Eudo Dapifer. They were all major landholders but none of them were important on that circuit, which was the pattern throughout the country. Commissioners

Below: Extracts from documents issued by William the Conqueror concerning lands belonging to the Abbey of Chertsey. Founded in 666, Chertsey was a favourite of William's, and in the first four lines he confirms the abbey's possessions, specifically Chertsey, Egham Thorpe and Chobham which meant that they did not have to pay taxes to the King. The middle two lines are a notification that William sent to his officials in Surrey, informing them that he had granted the abbey the four estates mentioned in the first document. The final four lines are a notification issued by William II between 1087 and 1100, confirming to Chertsey Abbey all their property and possessions. These three documents appear together because in the 14th century copies of them were probably required for a court case.

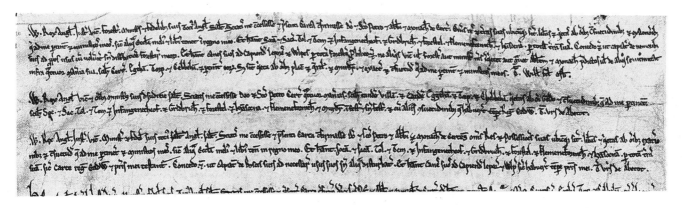

tended to be strangers in their circuits to prevent a conflict of interests, so that the information could be accepted as accurate by all parties. There were occasional disagreements over the value of estates, but the bulk of the arguments centred on the title to land. They were sorted out by hearings that the commissioners heard in the main town of the county involved. These hearings were long-drawn-out affairs and sometimes not all the cases had been heard by the end of the inquest. Where they were unable to come to a decision the commissioners took the land into the King's hands.

Once sufficient information had been gathered, the clerks who accompanied the commissioners produced a rough version of the description of their circuit. The bulk of the initial draft for the south western counties survives in the Cathedral Library at Exeter. From it we can see the trouble they had in arranging the copious details in their proper order. As extra facts came to light, and titles to estates were settled, so lines had to be added and amendments made. The sheer bulk of the resulting documents must have convinced those in charge that in order for the final description to be of manageable size a great deal of information would have to be left out.

Left: A hearing before the Domesday commissioners in the hall of a royal castle to consider a monastery's claim to an estate held by a Norman baron. In the body of the hall a group of monks are discussing their case with the jurors of the hundred in which the land lay. The commissioners, bored and frustrated, their table covered with scrolls and notes, gaze optimistically towards their clerks for guidance on the validity of the monks' claim.

Preparing the fair copy
Once the information on a group of shires had been drafted, the Exchequer officials at Winchester calculated how much parchment they would need for the final description. It is clear that the inquest proceedings were *still* going on while the final text was being inscribed, since space was left for entries which the clerk expected to receive but sometimes never did, while elsewhere extra lines had to be squeezed in. In the process of producing Domesday Book I, details of livestock were left out and many contractions and formulae used to save space. But for some reason, the descriptions of Essex, Suffolk and Norfolk were not shortened in this way; the clerks on that circuit produced a fair copy of a draft locally, possibly working in Bury Abbey, and this became Domesday Book II. The mistakes and unfilled spaces in both manuscripts, show that those responsible were working against time, and failed to complete their mammoth task before the seven month deadline; but it is a tribute to their skill and energy that they came as close as they did.

The Oath of Salisbury

On 1 August 1086 William arrived in Salisbury. There, within the fortifications today known as Old Sarum, Domesday Book was brought to him. All of the tenants-in-chief, and many of their sub-tenants, had gathered there and swore loyalty to William, and agreed that what was recorded in the great manuscript should be a true record of the land that they held. This ceremony marked the climax of the process which had begun at Gloucester, and was to be William's last public engagement as King of England. Having got the allegiance he sought from his English subjects he shortly afterwards left for Normandy, where he died a year later.

The departure of the King marked the end of the Domesday Inquest, and the text was sent to join other documents – and the royal jewels – in the Treasury at Winchester. At first Domesday consisted of a series of unbound booklets, but in due course these were bound together to protect them.

The Later History of Domesday Book

Although Domesday Book was kept in the Treasury it did not become a museum piece. The information it contained proved very useful to officials, and was used as evidence in court cases from the late 11th century onwards. In common with other government records in regular use it travelled with the King around the country.

Above: An aerial view of Old Sarum today. In the middle are the remains of the castle, while to the north west the ruins of the cathedral are visible. They were built in the late 11th century when the see of Sherborne was transferred here. Bishop Hereman ordered work to begin in 1078, though the cathedral was not completed till 1099. Before that Old Sarum was the remains of an old Iron Age fort. On 1 August 1086 William received the results of the Domesday Inquest here. It was Lammas time – a harvest festival (the word is a corruption of the Anglo-Saxon word 'loaf-mass'). After this, Sarum developed as the administrative centre of Wiltshire.

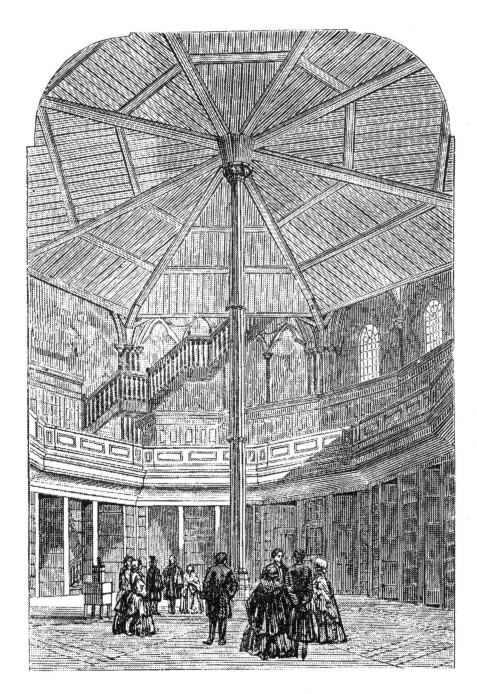

Right: The Chapter House of Westminster Abbey in use as a records office, prior to its restoration in 1865. At the dissolution of the monasteries in the 16th century the Chapter House was taken over to house Exchequer records that had accumulated in the Palace of Westminster. The fittings shown here were installed in the 1740s, and Domesday Book was kept in the Chapter House from shortly before 1775. It was removed in 1859 to the new Public Record Office in Chancery Lane.

At least three abbreviated copies of it were made in the 12th and 13th centuries, and as late as 1663 Domesday Book was sent to Gloucester to be exhibited in a court case. By the 17th century its use as a work of historical reference was becoming more common, and by the last quarter of the 18th century Domesday joined many other medieval documents in the Chapter House of Westminster Abbey when it was fitted up as a record office. In 1859 it moved to the new Public Record Office in Chancery Lane, where the volumes have been on regular display to the public since 1896.

Hundᵭ de Rocheford. Rageneiā tenet Sueñ in dñio q̄ uno
oꝛail. ⁊ p̄ .v. hiđ. Tc̄ .ii. car in dñio ᵹt .iii. Sep̄ .x. car hoꝳ. Tc̄ .xxi.
uill̄. m̄ .vi. Tc̄ .vi. boꝛđ. m̄ .xv. Sep̄ .ii. ſer. .x. ac̄ p̄ti. Silu̅ ᴄl poꝛc̄ m̄
.ii. pareꝰ. ⁊ vi. arpenni uineᷓ. ⁊ reddit .xx. modios uini ſibene procedit
Tc̄ .iiii. runc̄. ⁊ xiii. ań. .xxv. poꝛc̄. cv. ou̅. m̄ .v. runc̄. ⁊ .ii. pulli.
⁊ xx. ań. ⁊ xi. poꝛc̄. ⁊ lxxx. ou̅. ⁊ xvi. cap̄. Tc̄ ual .x. lib. m̄ p̄t unum
tanaindē. ⁊ in hoc manerio fecit Sueñ ſuū caſtellū. De hoc manerio
tenent .iiii. franci .ii. hiđ. ⁊ .iiii. car. ⁊ .iiii. boꝛđ. ⁊ ual .lx. ſol m̄
eoᵭ p̄tio.

Ragheleiam tenet .S. in dñio q̄d tenuit .i. lib̄ hō .t.r.e. p̄ oꝛań. ⁊ p̄
.ii. hiđ. ⁊ diᵐ. Sep̄ .ii. car in dñio. tc̄ .iii. uill̄ m̄ .ii. Tc̄ .v. boꝛ m̄ .vii.
hᷓnt tc̄ .ii. car ⁊ diᵐ. m̄ diᵐ tantū. Tc̄ .i. runc̄. ⁊ .ii. ań. ⁊ xv. ou̅.
m̄ .ii. runc̄. ix. ań. ix. poꝛ .xx. ou̅. Tc̄ ⁊ p̄ ual .xxx. ſol. m̄ .xl.

Hocheleiam tenent .ii. franci de Sueno. Godeboldꝰ .i. hiđ. ⁊ Odo
.xxx. ac̄. ꝫ hoc oꝛań tenuit .i. lib̄ hō .t.r.e. Sep̄ .ii. car. ⁊ diᵐ in dñio.
Tc̄ .iii. boꝛđ. m̄ .v. Tc̄ .v. ſoꝛ. m̄ .iiii. Paſt̄ ᴄ ou̅ Sep̄ .i. moł. tc̄ .v.
ań. ⁊ x. poꝛc̄. ⁊ c. ou̅. ⁊ .vii. cap̄. m̄ .i. runc̄ ⁊ xii. ań. ⁊ xvii. poꝛc̄.
⁊ c. ou̅. ⁊ iii. uaſa ap̄. Tc̄ ual .xxx. ſol. ꝫ m̄ .xl.

Eſtuuidā tenet Sueñ in dñio q̄d tenuit pat̄ ſuꝰ .t.r.e. p̄ uno
oꝛań. ⁊ p̄ iiii. hiđ. ⁊ diᵐ. Sep̄ .iii. uill̄. ⁊ .ii. car in dñio. tc̄ .vii. car
hoꝳ. m̄ .v. tc̄ .xxi. boꝛ. m̄ .xxx. Sep̄ .ii. ſer. iiii. ac̄ p̄ti. Tc̄ ſilu̅
.l. poꝛc̄. m̄ .xxx. m̄ .i. moł. Paſt̄. ᴄᴄᴄ. ou̅. Tc̄ .ii. runc̄. ⁊ .vi. ań.
xxx. poꝛc̄. ᴄᴄᴄ. ou̅. m̄ .ii. runc̄. ⁊ .ii. pull̄. ⁊ xxxiii. ań. xl.
poꝛc̄. ᴄxxxvi. ou̅. Tc̄ ual .vi. lib. m̄ .xx. De hoc manerio

Photograph of folio 43b of Domesday Book Volume II

This describes some of the Essex estates of Suen, a tenant-in-chief. Although only three counties are described in this volume of Domesday, a page from it has been selected in preference to one from Volume I because the fuller information gives a better picture of England at the time.

ESSEX

Line 1   **Hundred** *of Rochford. Suen holds Rayleigh in demesne as one* [1] [2]

Line 2   *manor and 5 hides. Then* [3] *2 ploughs on the demesne, now 3. Always 10 ploughs belonging to* [4] [5]
      the men. Then 21 [6]

Line 3   *villeins, now 6. Then 6 bordars, now 15. Always 2 slaves. There are 10 acres of meadow, and wood for 40 pigs. Now*

Line 4   *1 park, and 6 arpets of vineyard, which produce 20 muids of wine if it does well.* [7] [8]

Line 5   *Then 4 horses, 13 animals, 25 pigs, 105 sheep; now 5 horses, 2 colts,* [9] [10]

Line 6   *20 animals, 11 pigs, 80 sheep, and 11 goats. Then it was worth £10, now the same without counting the wine.*

Line 7   *In this manor Suen has built his castle. Of this manor*

Line 8   *4 Frenchmen hold 2 hides, with 4 ploughs and 4 bordars, worth 40/− of the*

Line 9   *above total.*

Line 10   **Suen** *holds Rayleigh in demesne (it was held in King Edward's time by a freeman) as one manor and* [11]

Line 11   *2½ hides. Always 2 ploughs on the demesne. Then 3 villeins, now 2. Then 5 bordars, now 6.*

Line 12   *These men had then 2½ ploughs, now only a half. Then 1 horse, 2 animals, and 15 sheep.*

Line 13   *Now 2 horses, 9 animals, 9 pigs, and 20 sheep. Then and after the Conquest it was valued at 30/−, now for 40/−.*

Line 14   **Hockley** *is held of Suen by 2 Frenchmen: Godebold has 1 hide, and Odo* [12]

Line 15   *30 acres. This manor was held by a freeman in the time of King Edward. Always 2½ ploughs on the demesne.*

Line 16   *Then 3 bordars, now 5. Then 5 slaves, now 3. There is pasture for 100 sheep. Always 1 mill. Then 5*

Line 17   *animals, 10 pigs, 100 sheep, and 7 goats. Now 1 horse, 13 animals, 22 pigs,*

Line 18   *100 sheep, and 4 hives of bees. Then valued at 30/−, after the Conquest and now 40/−.*

Line 19   **Eastwood** *is held by Suen in demesne (in King Edward's time it was held by his father), for a* [13]

Line 20   *manor and 3½ hides. Always 3 villeins, and 2 ploughs on the demesne. Then 8 ploughs*

Line 21   *belonging to the men, now 5. Then 21 bordars, now 30. Always 2 slaves. There are 4 acres of meadow. Then there was wood*

Line 22   *for 50 pigs, now for 30. Now 1 mill, and pasture for 300 sheep. Then 2 horses, 6 animals,*

Line 23   *30 pigs, and 300 sheep. Now 2 horses, 2 colts, 33 animals, 40*

Line 24   *pigs, and 136 sheep. Then valued at £6, now for £10. Of this manor* [14]

1. Tenant-in-chief.
2. Suen farmed it himself, and had not let it to a sub-tenant.
3. Its assessment for the *geld* – a national land tax.
4. 'Then' refers to the day of King Edward the Confessor's death in 1066; 'now' means 1086 when the survey was undertaken.
5. The land farmed by Suen, as distinct from the land farmed by the villeins and bordars (6).
6. *(see footnote 5)*
7. French term for measuring extent of vineyard.
8. Measure of volume.
9. Rounceys, or pack horses.
10. Probably cows.
11. Another holding in the village.
12. These were probably two of Suen's knights.
13. Robert fitz Wimarc, a Breton relative of King Edward's, who lived in England for a number of years before the conquest. He built a castle at Clavering in west Essex.
14. See pages 26–27 for illustration of Rayleigh.

Chapter  3

The Ruler and the Ruled

The most striking impression which even a superficial study of Domesday gives is of the unequal distribution of the nation's wealth. This is emphasized by the fact that within each county the estates of individual barons were all listed together. Of the 1400 tenants-in-chief in all England only 180 had land worth more than £100 a year and, of those, 10 men held a quarter of the entire landed wealth of England. In the county of Essex, half of the land in lay hands was held by five individuals. This concentration of wealth and power was a deliberate act by William, and one which helped to maintain the stability of his government. When assessing the wealth of the community it is difficult to compare the values of Domesday England with those of today, but we know that in 1086 a man with an income of £10 a year was thought to have a good income.

The coming of the Normans was accompanied by the introduction of the feudal system. All the land in England was now the property of the King, and he allowed others to hold some of it in return for providing him with certain services. These included not only customary payments of cash, but also the provision of a fixed number of knights when the King wanted them to serve in his army. The individuals and church institutions who held land directly from the King are referred to as tenants-in-chief. Often they sub-let parts of their land to others in return for some of the dues which would help them

Below: This detail from the Bayeux Tapestry shows King William conferring with two of his leading advisers, who were also his half-brothers. To his right sits Bishop Odo (see pages 4–5) and to his left Robert Mortain. They were the largest lay landowners after the king and had the status of tenants-in-chief.

Right: A diagram showing the structure of England's feudal society, based on records for the county of Huntingdonshire in 1086. At the top of the scale is the King, from whom all land and rights are ultimately derived. On the level immediately below him are the tenants-in-chief, who hold their land direct from the King. In Huntingdonshire there are 35 individuals and church institutions in this category. The third level consists of the 66 men who hold land from the tenants-in-chief. The fourth level contains three groups who, although broadly similar in their position in society as a whole, vary considerably in their economic status. The easiest to describe are the knights, the armed retainers of the tenant-in-chief, maintained by him to discharge his military obligations to the King. Burgesses are town-dwellers, who derive the bulk of their income from trade and/or manufacturing. Some of them have small-holdings, which are cultivated for them by bordars (fifth level). Sokemen are also small-holders, whose land is not strictly part of a manor, although they owe their lord (often the lord of the nearest manor) certain dues in the form of money and services. The majority of the inhabitants of the county were villeins, men who lived in villages, farming perhaps 30 acres (12 hectares) of land, and owning a few plough oxen. At the bottom of the social scale, four removes from the King are the bordars, many of them probably freed slaves, with about five acres (two hectares) of land each. Although Huntingdonshire is unusual in that no freemen or slaves are recorded, the county otherwise contains a good cross-section of population groups. Its 47 priests are not mentioned on the chart since they varied in status from freemen to villeins.

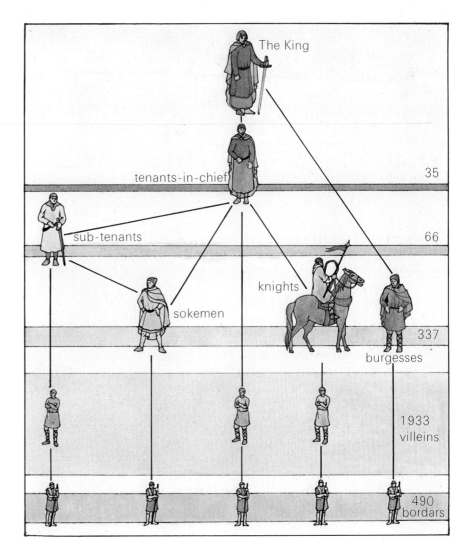

discharge their obligations to the King – granting land to their knights, for instance, which they held in return for military service. An ambitious tenant-in-chief with a network of tenants and retainers could have posed a threat to the King himself, and William took the precaution of making sure whenever possible that a baron's estates were not close together, but scattered about the country so that his influence was dispersed.

In all, Domesday Book mentions 107 different groups and classes of people (including a hunter, 111 Welshmen, two bee-keepers, a poor woman, and five potters!) The diagram shows the shape of the Domesday population of Huntingdonshire, and it is important to note that the figures refer to heads of households rather than to individuals, so the total population of the county in 1086 is likely to have been at least four times larger than the 2914 individuals recorded in Domesday Book. Based on the figures from all the counties the total population of England is estimated to have been at least 1¼ million.

Domesday England

Life in the countryside

The rhythm of life in the countryside was dictated by the seasons, and the cycle of work on the land. In the summer months everyone worked as hard as they could to gather in the harvests of corn, vegetables, fruit, and hops. As the days shortened into autumn, the land was manured by the flocks and herds brought in from their summer grazing, and then ploughed. Breeding animals were selected, and the rest slaughtered, their hides sold, and the meat preserved for the winter. During the winter, fences and buildings were mended, and other repairs carried out. In the spring the seed was sown and the animals let out into the meadows again.

The villeins, bordars, and slaves who did the farm work were obliged to spend varying amounts of time labouring on the lord's

The countryside at harvest time. This was a busy time of the year for the miller. A cart can be seen bringing in bags of grain for grinding, while two other carts have left the mill loaded with flour. One of them has used the ford to cross the river and is heading off towards another village. A man with a sickle goes out to continue cutting the corn in the field near the mill, while a slave is seen ploughing nearby. The isolated houses of cottars are to be seen near the ford, and beyond the mill. The villeins' homes are dotted

around the village green, at the end of which lies the thatched church, which boasts a pre-Conquest round tower. This water-mill is equipped with an overshot wheel. To work it, the river must be dammed some distance away so a reservoir is formed. From there, water is led to the top of the wheel through a channel called the head-race. The weight of the water in the mill's 'buckets' turns the wheel. The wheel, attached to an axle which, through a series of gears, turns the mill stones, thus mills the grain.

land. They also had time in which they could cultivate their own strips and attend to their livestock. Sometimes they were able to earn some cash by doing paid work on their own manor or elsewhere. At harvest time the lord of the manor supplied refreshments to all of the tenants gathering in his crops, probably pork, chicken, cabbages, eggs, cheese and apples. However, life in the countryside was hard and breaks from the usual routine were greatly valued. Sunday was a day when no work was done, and Monday too was often a day of rest. Other days off were the main festivals (Holy Days) of the church – Easter, Whitsun, Michaelmas, Christmas, and certain feasts of the Virgin Mary and other saints. These were marked by colourful processions round the village, with robed clergy, and acolytes bearing candles and ringing bells.

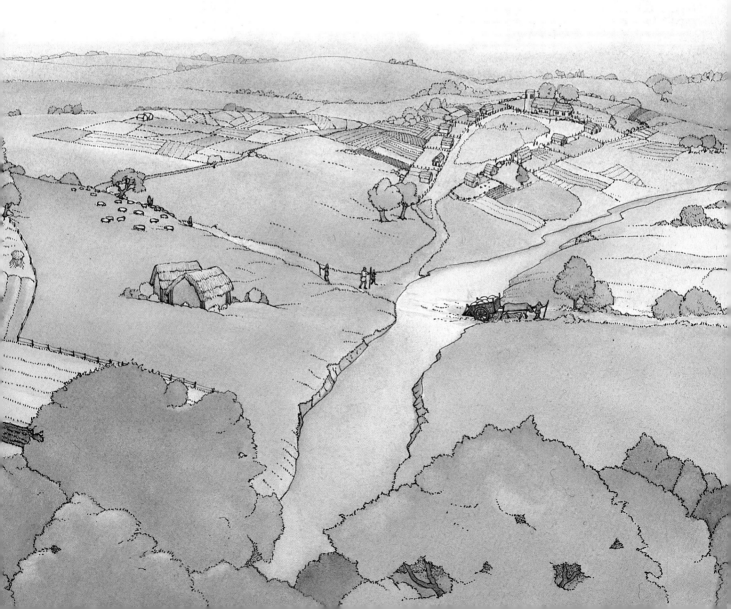

Domesday England

The social life of the village revolved around the parish church, not because the people were very religious, but because the church was the only public building. Not only were there the celebrations of the Mass, in which those present played the part of an audience rather than a congregation, but the church and churchyard were also used for fairs and games. Court sessions and other formal gatherings were sometimes held in churches too. Other recreations included drinking, hunting and trapping although these were usually reserved for the lord of the manor or the King.

Below left: Sheep grazing on the rich grass of Romney Marsh — a a typical scene at many coastal locations in Domesday England. In summer large flocks of sheep were run on the marshlands, their owners receiving a good return from the sale of their wool, meat, and the cheese made from their milk. In the background is the 13th century church of St Clement, Old Romney.

Below: The Nottinghamshire village of Laxton, ten miles north west of Newark, is one of a handful that still has unenclosed medieval fields. Recognizable from the strips of different crops growing in them, they can be seen in this aerial photograph in the foreground and in the background (right). At the time of the Domesday survey one whole large field would have been left fallow, while crops were grown in the others.

The Manor

The 11th century counterpart of a modern farm was the manor. But whereas the fields of a modern farm are often close together and quite distinct from their neighbours, this was not the case 900 years ago. The arable land in each village was divided into two or three large fields, which were further divided into strips. If, as sometimes happened, there was only one manor in the village, all of the arable land would belong to it, although it would not all be farmed by the lord himself. Some would belong to the villeins and bordars who laboured on his demesne. More often than not there was more than one manor in a village, in which case the large open fields were divided between the lords and their respective peasants. Sometimes there were strips which belonged to manors some distance away from the village. In addition to the land in cultivation, there was often pasture, meadow and woodland included in the manor.

Although at the time of Domesday Book the manor was the basic agricultural unit, it varied greatly in size and complexity. Some manors were very extensive, covering many square miles, whereas others amounted to only a few acres. In eastern England many manors had freemen and sokemen as well as land attached to them, and their dues and services contributed to the lord's income from the estate. Whatever the size and complexity of the manor it was the profits from a lord's manors which in large measure determined his position in society, and the extent of his influence.

Above: Two beehives. Made of basket-work, hives of this type are known as skeps, and were common in north west Europe and the British Isles. Because the bees need to be kept warm, the skeps are often placed in specially-built shelters, or recesses in outside walls.

Left: A bordar's house in a woodland clearing. The early years of Norman rule in England saw the clearing of areas of woodland to provide additional land for arable farming. In some areas bordars are encouraged to carve small-holdings out of the woods. Constructed of timber framing in-filled with wattle and daub (mud and plaster on a wicker frame), the house has a run for pigs attached to the end of it. The stump of a recently-felled tree is visible in the foreground, while chickens peck in the rough grass.

Domesday England

An aerial view of a Domesday manor, loosely based on the Domesday entry describing the Essex manor of Rayleigh, which belonged in 1086 to a baron named Suen (see pages 18–19). He built a castle (1) in his manor, and lives in the large thatched building (2) in its bailey. The farm buildings (3), and the house of the bailiff (4) who manages the agricultural side of the estate, are to be seen on the right. They include barns and a blacksmith's shop (5). Between them and the castle is an orchard (6). The arable land is divided into three fields, of which only two are under cultivation—the one beyond the castle, which grows wheat (7), and the one between the village and the orchard which grows barley or oats (8). The third, to the right of the second, remains fallow

(9). The villeins' houses (10) are clustered around the parish church (11), and both are, for reasons of privacy, at some distance from Suen's castle. In addition to his fortified home he has also made a deer park (12), and planted a vineyard in his manor (13).

Farming

The majority of the medieval workforce laboured on the land, since there were few mechanical aids. Ploughing was done by an iron-shared wooden plough pulled by a team of eight oxen. All other operations – sowing the seed, weeding the young plants, and harvesting – were done by hand. Men (and probably children) with slings were even employed to discourage birds from eating the crops (see illustration below).

Pastoral farming (livestock farming) was an important feature of the rural economy of Domesday England, although in many instances the livestock belonging to the villagers outnumbered those of the lord. The most common animals were sheep, who often spent the summer grazing on coastal marshes. It was not unusual to find pieces of marshland belonging to manors some distance from the coast. Pigs were the second most popular animal. They were kept in woods and fed on acorns. Indeed, in Domesday Book woods were often described in terms of the number of pigs that could be kept in them. Goats (kept for milk), cows, cattle, and horses were also reared, although the latter were either used as pack animals, or ridden by the aristocracy and knights. Beehives were common, the bees being kept not only for their honey, but also for the wax from the combs which was used to make candles. In the absence of sugar, honey was also used as a sweetener and to make mead.

Most of the industries mentioned in Domesday Book were agriculture-based, and often included within the manor. The

Above: Two types of boat in common use in Domesday England. At a time when transport on land is usually slow, and sometimes impossible in bad weather, bulky goods are often carried by water. Smaller rowing boats are used to ferry passengers and livestock across rivers.

Above: A hunting scene from the Bayeux Tapestry. On the left a man blowing a horn drives a pack of dogs towards a deer, which has been caught by another hound coming from the right. The second cartoon (below) shows springtime farm work. First the soil is ploughed, apparently by a horse-drawn plough, although normally oxen are used. The seed is then sown broadcast, after which a harrow covers it with soil. A man with a sling is employed to discourage birds from eating the seeds. The Bayeux Tapestry is in fact a piece of embroidery not a tapestry, probably made in Kent in the 1070s. It tells the story of the Norman Conquest of Britain, and in its lower margin are included these two views of contemporary English rural life.

most important and valuable industrial plant on a manor was the mill (see pages 22–23). Often it was built by the lord of the manor to grind not only his own corn, but also (for a charge) that of his villagers, and perhaps the harvest from neighbouring estates as well. Sometimes the mill was rented out to the miller, whose rent included a render of eels, which were caught in the weir across the river from the mill. Other fisheries existed on rivers, and a proportion of the catch was always paid to the lord of the manor.

Fish was eaten on Fridays and Holy Days, and salted for consumption during the winter. Salt itself, although mined in Cheshire and Worcestershire, was for the most part produced around the coast from evaporated sea water. Meat was also preserved using salt, since in the autumn many farm animals were slaughtered to reduce the pressure on scarce winter fodder. Once preserved, the meat was stored away to be eaten over the long winter months when fresh food was hard to come by.

Although there are occasional references in the Domesday text to other industries, the information it contains on activities such as quarrying, brick- and pottery-making, cloth manufacture, wood and metal working, and other processes which use natural or agricultural products is clearly far from complete. This was probably because the people who worked in these industries did not readily fit into the manorial pattern, or else because they are described in the text by their status in society rather than by their occupation.

Domesday England

A hunting party in the New Forest. The King and some of his barons are out hunting boar using a pack of hounds. Although hunting was popular with the aristocracy before 1066, the Normans have been responsible for the creation of forests – that is areas of countryside, *not necessarily wooded*, in which game has been preserved for hunting. Some of the Norman barons established parks on their estates. These are fenced-in areas of woodland and grazing in which deer are bred. William the Conqueror is a keen huntsman, and the *Anglo-Saxon Chronicle* says of him that he loves the stags as if he were their father. Other than the stag, 'beasts of the chase' were the buck, deer and fox; 'beasts of the forest' were the hart and hind, and 'beasts and fowls of the warren' were the hare, rabbit, pheasant and partridge. It was forbidden for anyone to enter a royal forest with bow, arrow, dogs or greyhounds without a special warrant and the clergy were also supposed never to hunt or hawk.

Domesday England

Living in a Town

In 1066 the invading Normans found a network of thriving and prosperous English urban settlements. Some of these towns had been founded by King Alfred in the 9th century, and were originally intended as fortified refuges during Viking attacks. The security provided by their earthen fortifications, and their strategic locations on main roads, encouraged the development of markets within them, and a period of economic growth continued until 1066.

The Domesday commissioners had varied success in describing towns, and a number were either omitted altogether (like London and Winchester) or only sketchily recorded (Bristol). It is clear that their terms of reference were vague as to what information was required and the multitude of tenancies within them made them difficult to interpret in feudal terms. Nevertheless, over a hundred towns are mentioned in Domesday Book. They range in size from large regional centres such as York, Lincoln, Norwich, and Oxford each with estimated populations of 4–5000, down to smaller local market towns, Totnes, Bodmin, and Guildford, whose inhabitants perhaps numbered less than 500.

In order to be successful, an early medieval town had to be situated on an important communication route, with an obvious catchment area around it, and not be too close to any neighbouring town. It was then set to develop as a market for the inhabitants of the surrounding countryside, craftsmen in the town itself, and travelling merchants. Although varying greatly in size and complexity, all towns contained at least some inhabitants whose only source of income was derived from selling manufactured goods; others had land in the fields at the edge of the town or extensive gardens within it. A typical town building consisted of a shop or workshop fronting on to the street, with living quarters behind. Some of these properties belonged to rural manors, and were used as an outlet to sell produce to the townspeople. The craftsmen who formed the town's permanent population sold leatherwork, cloth, metalwork, wooden containers and other specialized products that could not be made in the countryside. There would also be a mint where silver pennies, the basis of the nation's currency, were produced.

Most of the buildings in the town would have been made of timber, although a few – the mint, and town houses of senior clerics – were constructed of stone, and so too were the buildings of monasteries and nunneries which would still have been found in the town in 1086.

Towards the centre of the town, and often south of the main church, was the market place (see pages 34–35). This was a

Above: Colchester Castle. The largest Norman keep in Europe built by King William using the stones from the Roman town. Stone keeps had a number of advantages over timber ones. They could be built taller and wider and they did not catch fire so easily. The disadvantages were that the square corner towers could be attacked quite easily and the square shape narrowed the field of fire from the flanks.

Right: The stone keep of a large royal castle in the course of construction. At ground level a workman is busy mixing mortar, while carts arrive with supplies of timber and stone. The masons work from wooden scaffolding, attached to which is a pulley that is being used to raise baskets of stone. The walls (3–3.5 metres thick) are constructed with facings of squared blocks, and a mixture of rubble and mortar in between. On the roof of the corner turret the level of the battlements is being checked, while in the distance labourers are busy digging the ditch that will surround the keep (or tower) and other buildings that make up the castle. There will be one entrance.

A busy market place of an English town in the 1080s. To the left is the timber-framed market hall, which is used for official business, and for normal buying and selling. Around the edges of the square are shops, with living quarters behind them. Temporary stalls are erected in front of the shops. Dues had to be paid to the King or landowner as rent for a stall. In Domesday England selling was called 'cheaping' and in London the streets Cheapside and Eastcheap are a legacy from the days when markets were held there. Similarly any town prefixed by Chipping was a market town. Markets were usually held once a week, mainly for local produce, but once or twice a year great fairs would be held in the market place when foreign merchants brought their exotic linens and spices. Livestock, food, metal, leather, and wood work are the main types of goods sold. Entertainment is provided by dancing bears, jugglers and tumblers. Since the Norman Conquest a castle has been built in the town, which dominates the skyline behind the market place, and serves as a constant reminder of the new political order in England.

rectangular or triangular space in the centre of which stood the market hall. Around it, on market day, stalls would be erected and produce brought in from the outlying manors. Domesday Book only mentions 58 markets, although there must have been many more. Markets were an important source of revenue to the lord. He took fees from the stall holders, and a commission on sales. After the Conquest a number of new markets were established by the Norman barons. William Malet's market, held in his castle at Eye, ruined the Saturday market of the Bishop of Thetford at nearby Hoxne (both in Suffolk).

In Anglo-Saxon days towns had administrative as well as economic functions. The chief town of each shire would have been the venue of the shire court, the base from which the sheriff operated, and the site of his prison. Towns were regulated by burh courts which met three times a year to dispense justice and maintain order among the inhabitants, many of whom would not have been subject to manorial discipline. The administrative importance of towns was emphasized after 1066 by the construction of castles in many of them. These became the centres of royal and baronial administration in the area, and made obsolete the pre-Conquest town defences. Protected by the castles, the French merchants began to settle in English towns, often living together in separate communities.

There are signs that the towns suffered a good deal during the first 20 years of Norman rule. Domesday tells us of many instances where the invaders, seeing the obvious wealth of the English towns, greatly increased the dues that the inhabitants were required to pay to the King. Often a Norman was able to farm the revenues of a borough, in which case he kept anything that he was able to make over and above what the King expected to receive. At Norwich the render tripled between 1066 and 1086 from £30 to £90 a year, while in the year of the Inquest Wallingford was paying £80 although it was only valued at £30. These heavy demands seem to have ruined many of the burgesses, who left their homes and presumably returned to the country to work on the land. York had 540 empty houses, and in the Dorset boroughs over a third of the houses had been

Above left: '*King William sends friendly greetings to Bishop William and Geoffrey the Port-Reeve, and all the French and English burgesses of London.*' A translation of the first line of this notification in Anglo-Saxon that the King sent to the city at the time of his coronation on Christmas Day 1066. It means that the burgesses can continue to enjoy the laws and customs which were in force at the time of King Edward, and that every child is to be allowed to succeed to his father's property. The document, with its damaged seal (above), is preserved in the Corporation of London Records Office.

Above: The obverse (head side) of two silver pennies of William the Conqueror. Left: the two sceptres type minted between 1072 and 1074, and right: the later profile-cross and trefoils type minted between 1080 and 1083. Pre-Conquest arrangements for the production of currency continued with little change during the reign of William. There were mints in about 70 boroughs, and eight different types of pennies were issued in the course of his 21-year reign.

destroyed by 1086. The reasons for such losses are not always recorded. Sometimes it was the result of clearing ground for a new castle. With fewer inhabitants, and therefore higher taxes to pay, the lot of the English town dweller in 1086 was not an altogether happy one.

The Church

After the King and his barons, the most powerful institution in Domesday England was the church. Each village had its own parish church, and there were usually several in a medium-sized town. In many towns there were also religious houses of canons, nuns, and monks. The government of the church, like that of the state, was securely town-based, although its presence was also very evident in the countryside where over a quarter of the land belonged to the church. The fact that the bishopric and cathedral chapter of Winchester between them owned over 1000 plough-teams gives some idea of the enormous extent of their estates.

Above: An 11th century monastery, seen from the south. To the right of the church's central tower is the choir (1) where the monks hold regular services. To the left of the south transept (2) are the cloisters (3), where the young monks are instructed, and older ones write, study, and meditate. South of the transept is the chapter house (4), where the monks gather to discuss the running of the community. Beyond that is the dormitory (5), and along the south walk of the cloister the refectory (6) where they have their meals. The monastery precincts are surrounded by a wall, to cut off the monks from the town outside.

Domesday England

The basis of the wealth and power which the church enjoyed was the fact that it controlled the route to salvation. To ease their pathway to heaven kings and nobles lavished estates and other forms of wealth on religious houses. The church also played an important part in the secular government because most of those who could read were priests or monks. Bishops and abbots played important parts in royal council meetings not only because they were holders of large amounts of land, but also because they could read. The Norman 'civil service' consisted in the main of clerics. So closely were the ecclesiastical and lay governments intertwined that of the 18 bishops appointed to English sees between 1070 and 1089 eight of them were former royal clerks.

At Hastings William had fought under a papal banner, since he had received the Pope's blessing on his mission against the 'oath-breaker' Harold, and the wayward English church. The key difficulty for the pre-Conquest church was the position of Stigand, the Archbishop of Canterbury. After the flight of Archbishop Robert in 1052 Stigand was appointed in his place. With Robert still alive Stigand was condemned by the Pope, and few English bishops were consecrated by him. In April 1070 a church council at Winchester deposed him, and he was replaced by Lanfranc, abbot of William's foundation of St. Stephen's in Caen. While he was archbishop, Lanfranc began work on a steady programme of reform of the English church. A few bishops and abbots were removed from office, and as English prelates died they were replaced by Normans. By 1083 only eight English abbots were left in charge of the 20 most important monasteries.

With William's support Lanfranc held three councils, in 1072, 1075, and 1076. At them canons were approved to reform the church and bring it into line with current European practice. Castle and cathedral dominated the main towns, and represented the twin pillars of Norman rule – lay and spiritual. Married men were not in future to be ordained to the priesthood. A number of new priories were set up by the Normans, the most notable by William himself at Battle, the site of his victory over Harold. Others followed, and a number of Norman monasteries received grants of land in England.

At every level England was by now infiltrated by the Norman influence – the Anglo-Saxon heritage had begun to be replaced. After William's return to Normandy in 1086, work seems to have ceased on his great census. There was only one major addition after his death – a note of the lands given to the ancestor of Robert Bruce who became King of Scotland.

Above: The east end of the Abbaye aux Hommes in Caen, within which what remains of William the Conqueror's body is buried. He and his wife Matilda each founded an abbey on either side of the town of Caen. The site of the monastic buildings of William's foundation is now occupied by the Hotel de Ville (town hall), the fine 18th century façade of which can also be seen in the picture.

Glossary

ABBEY A monastery or nunnery, the head of which was an abbot or abbess.

ANGLO-SAXONS The English-speaking inhabitants of England who occupied the country after the collapse of Roman rule.

BAILIFF Steward or official of either a manor, or an administrative area. REEVE is another term with a similar meaning; the word SHERIFF is a corruption of shire reeve.

BARON Norman lord holding a large number of manors, deriving his powers from both the amount of land he held, and his closeness to the King.

CASTLE Fortified building, built by the King or one of his barons, and garrisoned by knights.

CATHEDRAL Large church in which a bishop had his throne or *cathedra*. Attached to the church was either a community of monks, or a group of priests.

CLERK Literally a priest, although in the 11th century the term was usually applied to a priest who was working for the government, for instance writing records such as Domesday Book.

COTTAR Unfree peasant, with either a garden or up to five acres (two hectares) of land, probably living in a cottage away from the village.

COUNCIL Meeting of the leading churchmen and lay barons, summoned by the King as and when he needed their advice.

COUNTY Area of local government, known before the Conquest as a SHIRE. In theory the territory of a count.

EARL Powerful landholder with administrative charge of several shires.

ESTATE Another name for MANOR.

EXCHEQUER Another name for the King's TREASURY. So called because the money and taxes due to the King were calculated using counters on a great chequered table.

FARM In Domesday England this did not refer to an area of agricultural production. A farmer paid the King a fixed annual rent or *farm* and was free to take whatever he could from the asset he rented which might be a borough or an estate.

GELD National tax, the usual rate of which was two shillings per hide.

HIDE Unit of tax (geld) assessment of an estate (varied from county to county). Similar to modern rateable values.

HUNDRED Unit of local government between the county and manor in size. Called *wapentakes* in the north.

LAY Not relating to the church; secular.

MANOR Unit of agricultural production, broadly similar to a modern farm.

MONASTERY Community of monks living together under a monastic rule.

NORMANS The inhabitants of Normandy, the area of northern France west of Paris. The aristocracy of the province were of Viking extraction.

NUNNERY Similar to a monastery, but members of the community were women.

PARCHMENT Treated skin of sheep or goat, used for writing on.

PRIORY Monastery or nunnery, headed by a prior or prioress. Less prestigious than an abbey.

RENDER Money and/or services and goods paid (rendered) by an estate or town to the King or its lord.

SEE The seat of a bishop, or where his cathedral is.

SHERIFF The senior royal official in a county, charged with its day-to-day administration, appointed by the King.

SLAVE Labourer who did most of the work on the lord's demesne. They did not normally have any land of their own, and had to be fed and housed at the lord's expense. A slave was not entirely without rights. He had some free time and could work for pay in it, occasionally accumulating enough to buy land and freedom.

SOKE An area within which the King had granted to a church or baron the right to try cases which would normally be heard in the King's courts. The owner of the soke also received the fines collected.

SOKEMAN Middle class peasant, similar to a freeman, but more closely tied to his holding. He lay in the soke of a lord, to whom he made customary payments.

SYNOD An assembly of the clergy convened to discuss church affairs.

TREASURY or EXCHEQUER The part of the royal household and government concerned with finance. Originally the place where the King's crown, jewels, and other treasures were kept. Important documents like Domesday Book were kept there too.

VIKINGS Scandinavians who migrated to England, northern France, and elsewhere in the 9th and 10th centuries.

Index

Note: page numbers in *italics* refer to illustrations.